The Battle of Hamburger Hill: The History and Legacy of One War's Most Controversial Battles

By Charles River Editors

A picture of American soldiers inspecting the field after the battle

About Charles River Editors

Charles River Editors is a boutique digital publishing company, specializing in bringing history back to life with educational and engaging books on a wide range of topics. Keep up to date with our new and free offerings with this 5 second sign up on our weekly mailing list, and visit Our Kindle Author Page to see other recently published Kindle titles.

We make these books for you and always want to know our readers' opinions, so we encourage you to leave reviews and look forward to publishing new and exciting titles each week.

Introduction

A picture of American soldiers on the field after the battle

"We are in for some tough fighting ahead, but I feel we have never before been more capable of success than now. The NVA we are going to meet out there will be highly trained, well-equipped, hard-core troops who will stand and fight, especially when we get close to his base camps and supply depots." - Colonel John Hoefling, 2nd Brigade, March 1, 1969

The Vietnam War could have been called a comedy of errors if the consequences weren't so deadly and tragic. In 1951, while war was raging in Korea, the United States began signing defense pacts with nations in the Pacific, intending to create alliances that would contain the spread of Communism. As the Korean War was winding down, America joined the Southeast Asia Treaty Organization, pledging to defend several nations in the region from Communist aggression. One of those nations was South Vietnam.

Before the Vietnam War, most Americans would have been hard pressed to locate Vietnam on a map. South Vietnamese President Diem's regime was extremely unpopular, and war broke out between Communist North Vietnam and South Vietnam around the end of the 1950s. Kennedy's administration tried to prop up the South Vietnamese with training and assistance, but the South Vietnamese military was feeble. A month before his death, Kennedy signed a presidential directive withdrawing 1,000 American personnel, and shortly after Kennedy's assassination, new

President Lyndon B. Johnson reversed course, instead opting to expand American assistance to South Vietnam.

Over the next few years, the American military commitment to South Vietnam grew dramatically, and the war effort became both deeper and more complex. The strategy included parallel efforts to strengthen the economic and political foundations of the South Vietnamese regime, to root out the Viet Cong guerrilla insurgency in the south, combat the more conventional North Vietnamese Army (NVA) near the Demilitarized Zone between north and south, and bomb military and industrial targets in North Vietnam itself. In public, American military officials and members of the Johnson administration stressed their tactical successes and offered rosy predictions; speaking before the National Press Club in November 1967, General Westmoreland claimed, "I have never been more encouraged in the four years that I have been in Vietnam. We are making real progress…I am absolutely certain that whereas in 1965 the enemy was winning, today he is certainly losing." (*New York Times*, November 22, 1967).

At the same time, the government worked to conceal from the American public their own doubts and the grim realities of war. Reflecting on the willful public optimism of American officials at the time, Colonel Harry G. Summers concluded, "We in the military knew better, but through fear of reinforcing the basic antimilitarism of the American people we tended to keep this knowledge to ourselves and downplayed battlefield realities . . . We had concealed from the American people the true nature of the war." (Summers, 63).

Faced with such a determined opponent, skilled in asymmetrical warfare and enjoying considerable popular support, the Americans would ultimately choose to fight a war of attrition. While the Americans did employ strategic hamlets, pacification programs, and other kinetic counterinsurgency operations, they largely relied on a massive advantage in firepower to overwhelm and grind down the Viet Cong and NVA in South Vietnam. The goal was simple: to reach a "crossover point" at which communist fighters were being killed more quickly than they could be replaced. American ground forces would lure the enemy into the open, where they would be destroyed by a combination of artillery and air strikes.

One of the most infamous battles of the Vietnam War, the Battle of Hamburger Hill – officially, part of Operation Apache Snow – occurred in spring of 1969. Towering over the perilous, elephant grass choked length of the A Shau Valley, Hill 937, otherwise known as Hamburger Hill or Dong Ap Bia ("Crouching Beast Mountain"), rose to a height of over 3,074 feet above sea level. The Americans launched a series of 11 attacks against this low mountain's NVA defenders, leading to fierce combat involving both advanced weaponry and infantry tactics unchanged since World War II.

The Battle of Hamburger Hill ranks as one of the most famous – or infamous – of the Vietnam War. Over time, however, all nuance and context have vanished, leaving a legend of pointless butchery which ignores the very real strategic and tactical considerations that converged to produce the encounter. The battle pitted several battalions of the 101st Airborne Division, one of America's most famous fighting units, against the 29th Regiment of the NVA. The latter's toughness, skill, courage, and zeal earned it the unofficial sobriquet of "The Pride of Ho Chi Minh." Both units fought extremely hard and with great determination, inflicting high casualties on one another.

The change from an elusive strategy to one of aggression marked a shift in North Vietnamese action, too. Documents captured during the battle indicated the 29th moved into the A Shau Valley and occupied Hill 937 as a staging area for a second full-scale attack on the city of Hue. This, in turn, triggered a shift in American military thinking, though as was often the case during the war, the results suffered from the effects of large-scale political interference.

The Battle of Hamburger Hill: The History and Legacy of One of the Vietnam War's Most Controversial Battles chronicles one of the most controversial campaigns of the war, and the effects it had on both sides. Along with pictures of important people, places, and events, you will learn about the Battle of Hamburger Hill like never before.

The Battle of Hamburger Hill: The History and Legacy of One of the Vietnam War's Most Controversial Battles

About Charles River Editors

Introduction

   The Start of the Vietnam War

   A Shau Operations Before the Battle

   The Start of the Battle

   Turning the Tide

   The Legacy of Hamburger Hill

   Online Resources

   Bibliography

Free Books by Charles River Editors

Discounted Books by Charles River Editors

The Start of the Vietnam War

"The last thing I wanted to do was to be a wartime President." – Lyndon B. Johnson

By the start of Operation Rolling Thunder, the United States had been heavily invested in opposing Vietnamese communism for the better part of two decades, and with the benefit of hindsight, the American war effort that metastasized there throughout the 1960s may seem like a grievous error and a needless waste of blood and treasure on an unwinnable and strategically insignificant civil conflict in a distant, culturally alien land. Indeed, it is still difficult for Americans today to comprehend how it was that their leaders determined such a course was in the national interest. Thus, it is essential at the outset to inquire how it was that a succession of elite American politicians, bureaucrats, and military officers managed, often despite their own inherent skepticism, to convince both themselves and the public that a communist Vietnam would constitute a grave threat to America's security.

Vietnam's first modern revolution came in the months of violence, famine, and chaos that succeeded World War II in Asia. Along with present-day Laos and Cambodia, the country had been a French colony since the late 19th century, but more recently, at the outset of World War II, the entire region had been occupied by the Japanese. Despite the pan-Asian anti-colonialism they publicly espoused, Japan did little to alter the basic structures of political and economic control the French had erected.

When Japan surrendered and relinquished all claim to its overseas empire, spontaneous uprisings occurred in Hanoi, Hue, and other Vietnamese cities. These were seized upon by the Vietnam Independence League (or *Vietminh*) and its iconic leader Ho Chi Minh, who declared an independent Democratic Republic of Vietnam (DRV) on September 2, 1945. France, which had reoccupied most of the country by early 1946, agreed in theory to grant the DRV limited autonomy. However, when the sharp limits of that autonomy became apparent, the Vietminh took up arms. By the end of 1946, in the first instance of what would become a longstanding pattern, the French managed to retain control of the cities while the rebels held sway in the countryside.

Ho Chi Minh

From the outset, Ho hoped to avoid conflict with the United States. He was a deeply committed Communist and dedicated to class warfare and social revolution, but at the same time, he was also a steadfast Vietnamese nationalist who remained wary of becoming a puppet of the Soviet Union or the People's Republic of China. Indeed, Ho's very real popularity throughout the country rested to no small extent on his ability to tap into a centuries-old popular tradition of national resistance against powerful foreign hegemons, a tradition originally directed against imperial China. As such, he made early advances to Washington, even deliberately echoing the American Declaration of Independence in his own declaration of Vietnamese independence.

Under different circumstances, Americans might not have objected much to a communist but independent DRV. The Roosevelt and Truman administrations had trumpeted national independence in Asia and exhibited almost nothing but contempt for French colonial rule. However, as Cold War tensions rose, and as the Soviet Union and (after 1949) Communist China increased their material and rhetorical support for the Vietminh cause, such subtle gradations quickly faded. Considering the matter in May 1949, Secretary of State Dean Acheson asserted that the question of whether Ho was "as much nationalist as Commie is irrelevant. All Stalinists in colonial areas are nationalists . . . Once in power their objective necessarily becomes subordination [of the] state to Commie purpose." (Young, 20 – 23).

Acheson

As a result, in 1950, the United States recognized the new puppet government France had established under the emperor Bao Dai, and by 1953 American financial aid funded fully 60% of France's counterinsurgency effort. When that effort finally collapsed in 1954, an international conference at Geneva agreed to divide Vietnam at the 17th parallel into a communist DRV in the north and an American-backed Republic of Vietnam in the south. Between 1955 and 1961, South Vietnam and its new president, Ngo Dinh Diem, received more than $1 billion in American aid. Even so, Diem proved unable to consolidate support for his regime, and by 1961 he faced a growing insurgency in the Viet Cong (VC), a coalition of local guerrilla groups supported and directed by North Vietnam.

Diem

Bao Dai

As Diem and (after a 1963 coup) his successors teetered on the brink of disaster, American politicians and military officers grappled with the difficult question of how much they were willing to sacrifice to support an ally. In 1961, President Kennedy resisted a push to mount air strikes, but he agreed to send increased financial aid to South Vietnam, along with hundreds (and eventually thousands) of American "military advisors."

The summer of 1964, which would normally be used to prepare for reelection, was a busy time for Lyndon B. Johnson's Administration. His attempts to steamroll ahead on domestic policy legislation were quickly sideswiped by a surprising foreign policy event in the Gulf of Tonkin. In 1964, the *USS Maddox* was an intelligence-gathering naval ship stationed off the coast of North Vietnam for the purpose of gathering information about the ongoing conflict between North Vietnam and South Vietnam. The borders between North and South, however, were in dispute, and the United States was less up to date on changes in these borders than the two belligerents.

In the process, the *USS Maddox* accidentally crossed over into North Vietnamese shores, and when the ship was sighted by North Vietnamese naval units, they attacked the *Maddox* on August 2, 1964.

Though no Americans were hurt, naval crews were on heightened alert as the *Maddox* retreated to South Vietnam, where it was met by the USS *Turner Joy*. Two days later, the *Maddox* and *Turner Joy*, both with crews already on edge as a result of the events of August 2, were certain they were being followed by hostile North Vietnamese boats, and both fired at targets popping up on their radar.

After this second encounter, Johnson gave a speech over radio to the American people shortly before midnight on August 4th. He told of attacks on the high seas, suggesting the events occurred in international waters, and vowed the nation would be prepared for its own defense and the defense of the South Vietnamese. Johnson thus had the Gulf of Tonkin Resolution drafted, which gave the right of military preparedness to the President without Congressional approval. The resolution passed shortly thereafter, giving the President the authority to raise military units in Vietnam and engage in warfare as needed without any consent from Congress. Shortly thereafter, President Johnson approved air strikes against the North Vietnamese, and Congress approved military action with the Gulf of Tonkin Resolution.

Once upon a time, Johnson had claimed, "We are not about to send American boys 9 or 10 thousand miles away from home to do what Asian boys ought to be doing for themselves." By the end of the year, however, over 16,000 Americans were stationed in South Vietnam. Regarding this about-face, Johnson would explain, "Just like the Alamo, somebody damn well needed to go to their aid. Well, by God, I'm going to Vietnam's aid!"

It would be years before the government revealed that the second encounter was no encounter at all. The government never figured out what the *Maddox* and *Turner Joy* were firing at that night, but there was no indication that it involved the North Vietnamese. Regardless, by 1965, under intense pressure from his advisors and with regular units of the NVA infiltrating into the south, President Lyndon Johnson reluctantly agreed to a bombing campaign, Operation Rolling Thunder, against North Vietnamese targets. He also agreed to a request from General William Westmoreland, the American military commander in South Vietnam, for the first American ground troops deployed to Vietnam: two battalions of Marines to guard the air bases.

Westmoreland

Years later, General Frederick Weyand speculated that the disingenuous pronouncements of officers and politicians, while instrumental in making the initial case for intervention, may have poisoned the well of long-term public support: "The American way of war is particularly violent, deadly and dreadful. We believe in using 'things'—artillery, bombs, massive firepower—in order to conserve our soldiers' lives. The enemy, on the other hand, made up for his lack of 'things' by expending men instead of machines, and he suffered enormous casualties. The army saw this happen in Korea, and we should have made the realities of war obvious to the American people before they witnessed it on their television screens. The army must make the price of involvement clear before we get involved." (Summers, 68).

Whether greater openness from the outset might have translated into steadier national resolve in the long term is impossible to say, but it would almost certainly have punctured some of the dangerous illusions that young American soldiers brought with them to Vietnam.

Compared with their predecessors in World War II and Korea, the average American soldier in Vietnam was considerably younger and in many cases came from more marginal economic backgrounds. The average American soldier in World War II was 26, but in Vietnam, the average soldier was barely 19. In part, this was due to President Johnson's refusal to mobilize the national reserves; concerned that calling up the National Guard would spook the public and possibly antagonize the Russians or Chinese, Johnson relied on the draft to fill the ranks of the military. Moreover, given the numerous Selective Service deferments available for attending college, being married, holding a defense-related job, or serving in the National Guard, the burden of the draft fell overwhelmingly on the people from working class backgrounds. It also particularly affected African Americans.

The American military that these young draftees and enlistees joined had been forged in the crucible of World War II and were tempered by two decades of Cold War with the Soviet Union. In terms of its organization, equipment, training regimens, operational doctrines, and its very outlook, the American military was designed to fight a major conventional war against a similarly-constituted force, whether in Western Europe or among the plains of northeast Asia. As an organization, the military's collective memories were of just such engagements at places like Midway, Normandy, Iwo Jima, Incheon, and the Battle of the Bulge. These campaigns predominately involved battles of infantry against infantry, tanks against tanks, and jet fighters against jet fighters. As boys, many of the young men who fought in Vietnam had played as soldiers, re-enacting the heroic tales of their fathers and grandfathers. The author Philip Caputo, who arrived in Vietnam as a young marine officer in 1965, recalled, "I saw myself charging up some distant beachhead, like John Wayne in *Sands of Iwo Jima*, and then coming home with medals on my chest." (Caputo, 6).

Expecting a simple conflict of good against evil and knowing little to nothing of the local culture, American soldiers in their late teens and early 20s arrived in Vietnam and found a world of peril, privation, and moral ambiguity. Despairing of and for young rookie soldiers like Caputo, Bruce Lawler, a CIA case officer in South Vietnam, virtually exploded with rage: "How in hell can you put people like that into a war? How can you inject these types of guys into a situation that requires a tremendous amount of sophistication? You can't. What happens is they start shooting at anything that moves because they don't know. They're scared. I mean, they're out there getting shot at, and Christ, there's somebody with eyes that are different from mine. And boom—it's gone." (Saltoli, 177).

Above all, success would be measured in terms of "body count," and Westmoreland's staff estimated the crossover point at a kill ratio of 10 Viet Cong to every American. To that end, officers rewarded soldiers for confirmed kills, rules of engagement were unofficially loosened, and operations were sometimes planned solely to increase the body count. As Philip Caputo notes, the consequences of such a strategy for the outlook of the ordinary American soldier were as tragic as they were predictable: "General Westmoreland's strategy of attrition also had an important effect on our behavior. Our mission was not to win terrain or seize positions, but simply to kill: to kill Communists and to kill as many of them as possible. Stack 'em like cordwood. Victory was a high body count, defeat a low kill ratio, war a matter of arithmetic. The pressure on unit commanders to produce enemy corpses was intense, and they in turn communicated it to their troops . . . It is not surprising, therefore, that some men acquired a contempt for human life and a predilection for taking it." (Caputo, xix).

Needless to say, this would affect the Battle of Hamburger Hill.

A Shau Operations Before the Battle

The A Shau Valley of Vietnam, sometimes referred to as "Mr. Victor Charlie's backyard" after the code-based nickname for the Viet Cong ("VC"), represented one of the routes by which North Vietnam moved men and materiel into the South. Thickly grown with both elephant grass and tropical forest, the inland valley featured extremely inhospitable terrain. A jumble of ridges, low mountains, gorges, and other gnarled, steep terrain rising thousands of feet above sea level made any attempt at maneuver a lengthy, crushingly exhausting process, and one that was subject to the constant risk of ambush.

Triple canopy jungle covered much of the higher ground, along with many of the lower areas of the valley. Besides the physical obstacle this forest presented – and the hordes of leeches found in its sodden recesses – it offered excellent cover to the Viet Cong and the soldiers lurking along its length. The thick rain forest foliage made aerial reconnaissance almost completely vain, while making close air support difficult even after establishing contact.

An American Huey in the A Shau Valley

The 25 miles of the valley ran roughly north to south, parallel to the coast and inland from several important South Vietnamese cities, including Hue. Due to its proximity to the Laotian border, the North Vietnamese used it as a route for infiltration of both men and supplies into the South. In fact, the infamous "Ho Chi Minh Trail" ran several branches over the mountain ridges into the valley itself, connecting up to primitive tracks and animal trails meandering through the dense jungle, bamboo, thorn, and elephant grass. Lieutenant Frank Boccia described the region's weather, recalling that "the heavy, relentless rains of the monsoon and later were, for the moment, a memory. In their place came a heavy, relentless sun, often glazed over by high thin clouds that served only to spread out the light and increase the humidity. In this respect, it was just like summer back in Washington; the same brassy pearl sky and the heavy heat, the same clinging moisture that became, after moments, unending sweat, the same hazy horizon." (Boccia, 2013, 110).

The valley housed a number of Montagnard tribes, along with an assortment of poisonous reptiles and a stunted subspecies of tiger, the Corbett's tiger, with a top weight of 400 pounds for mature males. This daunting environment increased the difficulty of American operations in the area many times over, ensuring that the North Vietnamese maintained control of much of the valley despite the American presence.

American forces started to enter the A Shau Valley as early as 1963, when American advisers accompanied South Vietnamese Army of the Republic of Vietnam (ARVN) units skirmishing endlessly with Viet Cong in the region. Soon, American Special Forces also commenced operations in the A Shau in support of the South Vietnamese. By 1965, the Special Forces set up an operating base and a satellite camp in the valley itself.

These installations naturally served as magnets for Viet Cong attacks. Severe assaults in March 1966 forced the Special Forces to evacuate by helicopter to avoid annihilation. Before retreating, their extremely courageous and skillful defense cost the Viet Cong as many as 1,000 killed, yet even at this early stage the American media portrayed the fight as an "ugly" and one-sided defeat. This effectively secured undisputed North Vietnamese control of the entire valley for several years.

Starting in April 1967, "Project Delta" long range reconnaissance patrols (LRRPs) probed the A Shau Valley once again. Most of these proved successful within their limits, providing the American military with a picture of the North Vietnamese activity there. However, the enemy noted these patrol and deployed counter-recon units, leading to a series of spectacularly vicious, yet little heralded actions amid the jungle, bamboo, and leech-infested elephant grass. The patrols successfully located huge North Vietnamese supply dumps, but MACV (US Military Assistance Command, Vietnam) failed to follow up on destroying these.

The events leading to Operation Apache Snow began in earnest with 1968's Tet Offensive. By the end of 1967, with nearly half a million troops deployed, more than 19,000 deaths, and a war that cost $2 billion a month and seemed to grow bloodier by the day, the Johnson administration faced an increasingly impatient and skeptical nation. Early in 1968, a massive coordinated Viet Cong operation - the Tet Offensive - briefly paralyzed American and South Vietnamese forces across the country, threatening even the American embassy compound in Saigon. With this, the smiling mask slipped even further, inflaming the burgeoning antiwar movement. Although American soldiers didn't lose a battle strategically during the campaign, the Tet Offensive made President Johnson non-credible and historically unpopular, to the extent that he did not run for reelection in 1968. By then, Vietnam had already fueled the hippie counterculture, and anti-war protests spread across the country. On campuses and in the streets, some protesters spread peace and love, but others rioted. In August 1968, riots broke out in the streets of Chicago, as the National Guard and police took on 10,000 anti-war rioters during the Democratic National Convention. By the end of the decade, Vietnam had left tens of thousands of Americans dead, spawned a counterculture with millions of protesters, and destroyed a presidency, and more was still yet to come.

Nearly 50 years after the campaign, the Tet Offensive continues to inspire impassioned and occasionally bitter debate among historians, military officers, government officials, veterans, journalists, and the public at large. Some consider the large-scale assault a strategic masterstroke that demolished American popular support for the war effort, while others consider it a catastrophic misstep that effectively broke the back of the Viet Cong guerrilla forces in South

Vietnam. Many claim the Tet Offensive exposed the Johnson administration's optimistic pronouncements as a deliberate pattern of lies and obfuscations designed to mislead the American public about the true nature of the war, but others blame anti-war elements and the media for mischaracterizing a substantial American victory as a shocking and catastrophic defeat. In the words of the historian Richard Falk, the Tet Offensive "remains a mirror for restating opposed preconceptions and validating contending ideological biases."

Indeed, despite some claims to the contrary, the ferocity and scope of the Tet Offensive appeared to have come as a massive shock to both the military command and the Johnson administration. Diplomat Richard Holbrooke, a member of the Johnson White House's Vietnam group who had earlier been an assistant to US Ambassador Henry Cabot Lodge, Jr. in Saigon, recalled, "There was an enormous confusion in the period from January 30, 1968, to March 30, 1968. Notwithstanding all the memoirs that have been written claiming that intelligence predicted the Tet offensive, the simple fact is that the Tet offensive caught the Administration unprepared. That's a fact. You can always go back later and find the intelligence that predicted [an attack], but we weren't ready for it in Washington. I was in [Undersecretary of State Nicholas] Katzenbach's office then, and I can tell you that there was horror and pandemonium all the way to the top. [Secretary of State Dean] Rusk and Katzenbach sent me out to Vietnam ten days later to make a personal assessment. I saw [Lodge's successor, US Ambassador Ellsworth] Bunker and [MACV commander General William] Westmoreland, and [Joint United States Public Affairs Office head] Barry Zorthian and [Deputy Assistant Secretary of State for East Asian and Pacific Affairs] Phil Habib and the others and with the exception of Habib, they were all in a state of shock, too." (Willenson, 149 – 50).

Under the circumstances, then, it is hardly surprising that American press coverage of the Tet Offensive and its fallout grew increasingly cynical, mistrustful of authority, and pessimistic. Even among historians and observers who believe that the prevailing narrative of the Tet Offensive has been badly misguided, and that it was actually a strategic victory for the Americans and South Vietnamese, it is generally acknowledged that the press response was at the very least an understandable reaction to the excessive optimism of the administration before the campaign.

In such a poisonous, confused atmosphere, official claims of an American victory in the Tet Offensive, whatever their merits, were bound to ring hollow. As Vermont Senator George Aiken declared, "If this is a failure, I hope the Viet Cong never have a major success." (Olson and Roberts, 186).

By late February 1968, with news of the Tet Offensive and the siege of Khe Sanh saturating the headlines, that number had plummeted to 32%, and by late March, it had fallen even further to just 26%. On March 10, popular anxiety was magnified when a *New York Times* article reported that in the wake of Tet, General Westmoreland had requested more than 200,000 reinforcements. This was somewhat misleading; Westmoreland had desired additional troops long before Tet, but not as a defensive measure. Instead, he had advocated taking the war to the enemy with massive offensives in both North Vietnam and Eastern Laos. With the Johnson administration unwilling to commit to the national mobilization that such an operation would necessitate, Westmoreland's proposal was a nonstarter. In February 1968, however, Joint Chiefs of Staff Chairman General Earle Wheeler apparently concluded that he could use the drama of Tet as a pretext to pressure Johnson to approve a large-scale mobilization that would include calling up the national reserves.

During the Tet Offensive, 10 battalions of Cong and NVA moved unseen through the A Shau Valley to pounce on Hue. While there, the NVA killed large numbers of civilians and executed 3,000 more, lending weight to the MACV supposition that the Viet Cong had been ordered to spearhead the offensive in order to wipe out tough, independent-minded fighters who might eventually turn into a resistance force against Ho Chi Minh.

The troops who took Hue and held it until dislodged during 25 days of fighting reached the city by way of the A Shau Valley. Similarly, the troops unsuccessfully besieging Khe Sanh approached it through the A Shau Valley as well. MACV and the Americans in general took note of these facts and realized the valley represented not just another supply route linked to the Ho Chi Minh Trail, but a superb jumping-off point for North Vietnamese attacks into South Vietnam.

General Creighton Abrams replaced General William Westmoreland as Army Chief of Staff, and following this, renewed interest in larger military operations in the A Shau Valley developed. Operation Delaware began on April 19th, slotted into a period when old French military records indicated a break in the doubled-up monsoons which typically occurred twice a year in the A Shau.

Abrams

The Americans successfully drove most of the North Vietnamese out of the valley during Operation Delaware, destroying a number of large supply dumps, 134,000 rounds of small arms ammunition, thousands of artillery shells, heavy weapons, and a single battered PT-76 amphibious tank. However, MACV did not permit the troops to remain, so the Americans airlifted out on May 25th, allowing the communists to enter the valley again and reoccupy their old positions. American losses included 142 killed in action and a number of aircraft shot down, while the North Vietnamese lost at least 869 killed.

Importantly for later operations such as Apache Snow, the Americans learned some of the constraints and possibilities of aerial actions in the A Shau. The French had not used helicopters in the manner of the Americans, relying on ground forces instead, so their conclusions about the weather had little applicability to American operations. As Lieutenant General John Tolson put it, "In other words, the forecast monsoon rains (which did occur) never produced theterrible flying conditions of low ceilings and scud which preceded them in April. An air cavalry division can operate in and around the scattered monsoon storms andcope with the occasional heavy cloudbursts far better than it can operate inextremely low ceilings and fog. [...] one must be very careful to pick the properweather indices in selecting an appropriate time for an airmobile operation. An inch of rain that falls in thirty minutes is not nearly as important as a tenth of an inchwhich falls as a light mist over 24 hours." (Tolson, 1999, 192).

In lieu of occupying the valley, the ARVN and American forces launched another major raid in August 1968, dubbed Operation Somerset Plain. The operation encountered only light resistance, with 7 Americans and 11 South Vietnamese killed. The official count of NVA dead amounted to 181. The Americans and South Vietnamese conducted as thorough a sweep as the terrain allowed, but they found only scattered supply caches containing paltry amounts of food and ammunition. The valley remained relatively quiescent and unoccupied after the drubbing delivered by Operation Delaware.

The immediate prelude to Apache Snow and the Battle of Hamburger Hill consisted of Operation Dewey Canyon. During this operation, Major General Raymond Davis led the 3rd Marine Division in a nearly month-long sweep of major portions of the A Shau Valley. The Marines entered the valley on January 22, 1969, using helicopters in imitation of Army airmobile operations. The official Marine history stated their objectives thus: "A victory, even against one or more limited objectives of minor or temporary tactical value, could have significant impact upon the civilian population, and a more far-reaching effect upon bargaining positions at the ongoing Paris Peace Talks. The enemy's jungle logistics system therefore would have to be destroyed before it could be used."

After establishing firebases in the valley, the Marines began sweeping the rugged terrain with patrols and soon found signs that the North Vietnamese might be planning to use the A Shau as a staging area again. One of these was an eight-building field hospital, fully equipped with Soviet-made surgical instruments, medicines, antibiotics, anesthetics, and other medical supplies. Signs indicated to the Americans that the North Vietnamese abandoned this hospital a few hours before their arrival. They also found a four-strand telephone link strung through the trees, emerging from Laos, crossing the entire width of the A Shau Valley, and disappearing over the ridges into South Vietnam.

Despite the hardships of the exhausting, muddy, leech-infested terrain, the Marines occasionally found a moment of pleasant respite, as Lieutenant Wesley Fox recounted: "A platoon a day went off the hill to a small river at the foot […] for swimming and fishing. Swimming and lying in the sun on a nice sandbar were great, but the real treat was the fish provided by the fishing expedition. The platoons would wind up their day at the river by throwing grenades in the deep holes and simply wading out and picking up the fish that floated to the top." (Yarborough,137).

As March began, encounters with the North Vietnamese picked up, and ambushes and platoon-scale combat erupted across the A Shau as Marines clashed with NVA regulars and Viet Cong. 1st Lieutenant Fox participated in one heavy firefight during which the entire company command except himself suffered wounds or died when a mortar round struck them. Fox, wielding his M16 rifle, killed an NVA sniper and machine gun team, then led A Company in a counterattack, joined by D company. This action left 105 dead NVA soldiers on the field, against 11 Marines killed during the fight. Fox, wounded multiple times, won the Medal of Honor.

While operating in the A Shau Valley, the Marines directly observed a steady stream of NVA trucks moving along roads just over the Laotian border. Due to restrictive rules of engagement, these vehicles remained off limits to attack, even though the United States theoretically supported the Laotian government fighting the Pathet Lao communist insurgents being supported by North Vietnam. With many of these convoys moving across the A Shau unobserved, the Marines requested permission to ambush enemy trucks inside Laos itself on the "highways" which entered South Vietnam through the valley.

Neither Creighton Abrams nor the White House approved this measure, so Colonel Robert Barrow authorized Captain David Winecoff to make a secret incursion across the border on February 22nd. Winecoff led Company H, 2nd Battalion, 9th Marines across the Laotian border to set up an ambush along Route 922. The ambush site included a vacant North Vietnamese bunker the Marines occupied.

The ambush proved successful. At 2:00 a.m., one NVA soldier walked through the ambush site, firing occasional AK-47 bursts into the roadside brush. None of his bullets came near the waiting Marines and they permitted him to pass unharmed. A single truck soon followed him, which the Marines likewise ignored.

Using a red flashlight, the Marine observation post alerted Winecoff that a convoy approached. The rumble of several truck engines broke the stillness. As the trucks entered the killing ground, Winecoff detonated several Claymore mines, which blasted out a swath of ball bearings in a cone in front of them, almost like a gigantic shotgun shell. The second truck in the convoy lurched to a stop, its driver riddled with steel spheres and killed instantly. Fire spouted up from its fuel tank and within moments the whole vehicle was ablaze, lighting up the Marines' targets.

Another Claymore struck the lead truck, damaging it heavily but missing the driver, who attempted to accelerate out of the ambush. However, one of the Marines in the bunker fired his M72 LAW (light anti-armor weapon), a 66mm rocket propelled grenade launcher. His round struck the first truck's cab, blowing it and the driver to pieces. The Marines hosed down the following trucks with their M16 rifles, while Winecoff called in an artillery barrage on Route 922. Loaded with ammunition, the trucks crashed, exploded, and burned.

Their mission a success, Company H fell back across the border into Vietnam. From the heights along the fringe of the A Shau Valley, they watched an undetermined number of ammunition trucks burning brilliantly in the Laotian night, racked by secondary explosions. Barrow managed to receive Creighton Abrams' authorization for the mission with a simple statement after it was already over via a radio to his superior: "Put another way, my forces should not be here if ground interdiction of Route 922 is not authorized." (Woodruff, 2005, 186).

During the rest of Operation Dewey Canyon, the Marines found a number of NVA caches and destroyed them, eliminating, among other things, over 800,000 rounds of 7.62x39mm AK-47 ammunition, 110 tons of rice, 16 artillery pieces, 104 machine guns, and 92 trucks. The operation cost 130 Marines their lives, while the North Vietnamese left 1,617 dead behind and carried off an unknown number of killed and wounded. The Marines helicoptered out on March 19th, 1969, officially ending Dewey Canyon.

The Start of the Battle

The operations that came before Apache Snow provide the context for the Battle of Hamburger Hill. The Americans repeatedly entered the A Shau Valley to disrupt North Vietnamese activity there, but never held the valley for any length of time. No top officials appeared interested in occupying the remote, rugged, inhospitable rain forest valley despite its value to the NVA and Viet Cong. Instead, officials authorized a series of incursions to destroy supply buildups and generally disrupt North Vietnamese activity there.

A Shau took on menacing significance during the Tet Offensive. After a division-strength unit seized Hue from the valley, the Americans viewed it not just as a supply infiltration point, but as a staging area for major NVA military operations. Moreover, while the Americans mostly drove the North Vietnamese out of the A Shau in 1968, leading to very low activity there for months, Operation Dewey Canyon revealed a fresh ramp-up of communist military activity there. The huge caches of ammunition, rice, and weaponry appeared to be signs of another imminent NVA attack out of the valley.

The high volume of truck traffic into the A Shau area – in many cases, along roads the NVA had actually paved in Laos to allow faster deliveries – meshed with intelligence that the elite 29th Regiment of the NVA had entered the valley. This persuaded the Americans that the North Vietnamese might be planning a second offensive against Hue and the nearby coastal cities in the immediate future. Aerial reconnaissance showed two more regiments moving towards the A Shau in Laos.

To quash this possibility, Operation Apache Snow began almost immediately after Dewey Canyon. The overall commander, Major General Melvin Zais, had experience in fighting against adversaries entrenched in mountainous positions from his World War II service. There, he had commanded forces dislodging the veteran German 34th Infantry Division from the Col de Braus in the Alps during Operation Dragoon in southern France.

Zais

Operation Apache Snow was one of three operations intended to drive the North Vietnamese out of the entire length of the valley. Operation Massachusetts Striker began in the southern valley on March 1st with the deployment of the XXIV Corps' 2nd Brigade. Helicoptered into a landing zone (LZ) and attempting to establish a firebase, these men came under heavy NVA attack. After several days of heavy fighting, during which air support and artillery helped the Americans beat off several determined North Vietnamese charges, the 101st Airborne Division troops secured "Bloody Ridge" or Dong A Tay, blasting the last NVA soldiers out of their spiderholes.

With the southern A Shau more or less secured, the second operation, Apache Snow, began in the north. Five battalions of troops in all participated in the initial incursion into the northern valley. These consisted of two ARVN battalions from the South Vietnam 1st Division, and three battalions of the 101st Airborne, the 1/506th, the 3/187th, and the 2/501st.

In preparation for the soldiers' arrival, a massive artillery bombardment of the selected Landing Zone (LZ) sites began at 7:10 AM on May 10th, 1969. Following this, a Cobra gunship arrived at each LZ to hammer the jungle and elephant grass nearby with minigun fire and rockets. Only after this hour and a quarter long preparation did the first troop transport helicopters arrive.

The North Vietnamese offered only very light initial resistance, with sporadic sniper fire being the only problem at most of the LZs. Once on the ground, and somewhat surprised by the lack of NVA activity, the Americans moved out in simultaneous reconnaissances in force (RIFs) both east towards the South Vietnam side of the valley and west towards Laos. The plan intended to force the North Vietnamese to fight – in which case, they would be destroyed – or retreat and allow the Americans to destroy their supply caches, weapon caches, and installations undisturbed. Secondary objectives included cutting or otherwise interdicting the North Vietnamese highways in the valley. Finally, the 3/187th, under the command of Lieutenant Colonel Weldon Honeycutt, had orders to secure Dong Ap Bia, Hill 937, due to its importance as a hub for the North Vietnamese supply trail network in the A Shau.

Honeycutt

Honeycutt was an abrasive, hot-tempered, aggressive commander who nevertheless won the grudging respect of many of his subordinates with his professionalism, toughness, and military skill. His Korean war prowess, which saw his rapid promotion from private to captain, earned him the nickname Tiger, and during the Battle of Hamburger Hill, he would also gain the sobriquet Blackjack after his radio call sign. His battalion, the 3/187th, had the name "Rakkasans," which means "the umbrella guys" in Japanese (a World War II nickname for paratroopers). He felt immense pride in the unit, believing them to be among America's finest soldiers. As such, he constantly badgered soldiers to live up to the standards he expected of them, seasoned by very little praise indeed.

Honeycutt and his command unit, together with Delta Company of the Rakkasans, moved directly to Dong Ap Bia. On one of the northern spurs of the looming, jungle-cloaked mass soaring into the sky above them, the approximately one hundred officers and men began clearing a new LZ, setting up defenses, and creating a command post. This new LZ would form the hub for the planned push to the summit of the Crouching Beast the following day.

A picture of injured 101st Airborne Marines being evacuated during the operation

In the meantime, Alpha and Charlie companies continued the reconnaissance in force as ordered. Almost immediately, their sweep found dozens of North Vietnamese huts and bunkers, some with cooking fires still smoldering. Large vegetable gardens stretched amid the elephant grass near many of these structures. Now on high alert, the Americans probed cautiously forward. Shortly afterwards, at 2:00 p.m., a recon helicopter flushed half a dozen NVA soldiers out of a still-occupied hut. Cobra gunships pounced, hosing down the fleeing troops from the air with their miniguns. Elsewhere, an NVA anti-aircraft gun opened fire on a helicopter, which managed to bomb it, resulting in an explosion that threw pieces of men and machine high into the air. Simultaneously, Honeycutt received numerous reports from other helicopters by radio that the terrain around Dong Ap Bia appeared thickly encrusted with enemy bunkers and housing.

Honeycutt called for the release of Bravo Company, the final element of his battalion, in hopes that they could safely reach the LZ before firing began. His superior, Colonel Joseph Conmy, immediately ordered Bravo Company aboard the helicopters and sent to Honeycutt's position, where his men still worked with chainsaws to complete the LZ. As Bravo company's 16 helicopters approached the LZ, Lieutenant Frank Boccia, a platoon commander, saw a spectacular mountain thunderstorm over part of the valley: "Then I saw, to the northeast, in the direction of Hill 1485, a thick, dirty grey blanket of clouds. Red flashes suddenly lit the interior of the cloud mass, turning the outer edges a deep mauve. I could see the rain and hail as it fell in raging sheets onto the valley floor below. [...] The lightning flashed and glowed, usually showing only as a red or purple smear within the clouds; occasionally it shone orange or yellow. [...] The thunder was constant; deep, booming waves of sound that washed over the puny roar of the helicopter engine as the surf washes over and obliterates a child's pool scooped out of the beach sand." (Boccia, 2013, 177).

The helicopters landed at 4:30 p.m., disgorging their cargoes of soldiers. Though Honeycutt had chosen correctly in having the troops arrive as soon as possible, they did not avoid all fire. Acting aggressively, the NVA worked close and fired at the helicopters with AK-47s, and, within a few moments, RPGs. Boccia recounted his feelings upon realizing the danger: "Pack! Pack! Pack! A hollow, snapping sound, from the trees. I hear it for the first time; the sound an AK-47 makes when it is fired directly at you […] We are underfire. Suddenly a sort of laughter bubbles uncontrollably from some unimagined place within me. For the briefest of moments, I feel a fierce joy at being young and alive and staring down the ancient tribal enemy." (Boccia, 2013, 178).

One of the UH-1 Huey helicopters crashed on the LZ, and a brief firefight ensued. Three men, including several of the helicopter crew, suffered wounds. The North Vietnamese also scored direct hits on one of the Bravo Company men and the helicopter's pilot with RPG rocket-propelled grenades, blasting both men into multiple gory chunks strewn over the area.

Two more helicopters crashed at the LZ several hours later while attempting to avoid small arms fire during their approach, forcing a temporary closure of the LZ and resulting in more casualties. Bravo company underwent these difficulties and eventually dug in on the high ground next to the LZ overnight, using salvaged M-60 machine guns to greatly strengthen their position. Meanwhile, the battalion prepared to advance up Hamburger Hill the next day.

When daylight returned to the A Shau Valley, Honeycutt radioed Bravo Company to move up the flanks of Dong Ap Bia. At this point, nobody on the American side knew that between 1,200 and 1,600 men of the 29th NVA Regiment and elements of other regiments awaited them on the mountain. The assumption remained that the North Vietnamese encountered the day before represented patrols or "trail watchers" only.

Captain Charles Littnan got his company moving, placing the 1st Platoon under the explosive tempered but highly reliable Lieutenant Boccia in the lead. The Rakkasans probed cautiously forward up narrow trails fringed by dense bamboo and vine-wreathed jungle. They grew even warier when they encountered dead NVA soldiers, numerous blood trails, and discarded equipment. Simultaneously, Honeycutt's interpreter – a turncoat North Vietnamese named Vinh, whom the Lieutenant Colonel called FT for "f***ing traitor" – informed Honeycutt that captured documents indicated the whole NVA 29th Regiment was in the area.

Bravo Company continued their RIF up the northern slopes of the mountain, halting for half an hour shortly after noon to eat their rations and sit out a brief, torrential rainstorm. The rain made the trail slippery and treacherous, slowing the already cautious and difficult climb further. Littnan, finally weary of Boccia's caution, ordered 4th Platoon under Lieutenant Charles

Denholm to leapfrog ahead and advance more quickly.

One of Denholm's men, Aaron Rosenstreich, found a communications wire strung in the bamboo, indicating a major NVA installation nearby. Meanwhile, the 1st Platoon of Alpha Company under Frank McGreevy found a major truck road northwest of Dehholm's position, concealed by tall jungle trees with their tops tied meticulously together to create an impenetrable canopy overhead. All signs pointed to large numbers of NVA troops somewhere in the area.

Advancing past the commo wire, Denholm's men ran into NVA in spiderholes at 2:00 p.m. The North Vietnamese opened fire, mortally wounding Rosenstreich and others firing into the men following him. The NVA soldiers showed considerable skill, popping out of their well-concealed holes at irregular intervals to let loose a burst of automatic fire before dropping down out of sight again.

The firefight ended with three Americans killed and seven wounded before Denholm and his men fell back down the trail with their casualties. Bravo Company radioed for a rocket strike from the nearest two Cobra gunships in the area, but unfortunately, these attack helicopters mistook Honeycutt's partially constructed command post for an NVA position. Rockets screamed in and blasted the Americans, strewing the ground with wounded and dying soldiers. Two men died outright, 12 more suffered serious wounds requiring evacuation, and 23 more sustained lighter injuries.

Honeycutt himself took a piece of shrapnel, which embedded itself deeply in his back. The piece of hot metal pressed on one of the Lieutenant Colonel's major nerves, causing intense pain and numbing both of his legs. However, he remained mobile, if barely, and refused evacuation. He would continue to command, but the excitable battalion commander flew into a towering rage at the friendly fire incident. Over the radio, he threatened to shoot down any aircraft that approached without his express permission. As he did so, a shower of 120mm mortar shells from an NVA battery in Laos struck the command post as well, showing that a competent North Vietnamese forward observer had eyes on the command group.

Prior to the friendly fire incident, Honeycutt had planned to pummel the ground ahead of Bravo company with artillery support, then order Littnan to continue the advance. However, the loss of his forward observer during the Cobra airstrike persuaded him to order Bravo company to withdraw and establish defensive positions. He then ordered Charlie Company and Delta Company to converge on Dong Ap Bia for a three-pronged advance in force.

With a few A-1 Skyraiders dropping 500 pound bombs upslope to deter any NVA advance, Bravo company retreated a short distance and dug in. Lieutenant Marshall Eward and two privates slipped back upslope to retrieve two of Bravo's M-60 machine guns left behind in the retreat. Covered by darkness, they carried out their mission successfully, but they saw and heard scores of NVA soldiers moving about and talking on the jungle-clad slope around them.

Taking advantage of the relatively quiet overnight hours and eschewing sleep, Honeycutt ordered a medevac for himself in the early morning of May 12th. Medics at Firebase Currahee dug the thumb-sized chunk of shrapnel out of his back, relieving pressure on the nerve so that he could walk again. A helicopter then flew him back immediately to the jungle LZ on the northern side of Hamburger Hill, arriving before sunup.

As the sun rose over the A Shau Valley, four A-1 Skyraiders buzzed in from the east to drop strings of 500 pound bombs and canisters of napalm close to the encounter site of the day before. They also strafed the jungle extensively with their 20mm cannons. Following this preparation, Littnan ordered Boccia and his 1st Platoon to advance to the combat site but to retreat should they meet stiff resistance.

The bombardment from the Skyraiders cleared enough of the jungle so that the leading soldiers of 1st Platoon, Bravo Company immediately spotted the low, sinister outline of a North Vietnamese log bunker ahead of them. Spec 4 Philip Nelson and another soldier set up a 90mm recoilless rifle and fired two rounds into the bunker, partially destroying it.

Like kicking over an anthill, this action roused scores of waiting NVA from their cover. Swarming from spiderholes and slit trenches, they fired waves of RPGs into the trees over the Americans so that a deadly hail of shrapnel and splinters blasted down onto their prone forms. Several more bunkers opened fire with heavy machine guns. One of the RPGs scored a hit on the recoilless rifle. Boccia explained, "I was looking directly at the 90mm team when, to my horror, an RPG hit directly in front of them. The black barrel of the gun went high in the air, emerging out of a cloud of dirt, leaves and explosives. I saw a helmet go flying; then Clifton and Nelson appeared, their bodies rolling down slope." (Boccia, 2013, 319).

Both Nelson and his assistant Clifton not only survived, but miraculously suffered no injuries whatever. Boccia ordered the 1st Platoon to fall back with their casualties, and F105 jets streaked in to blast the North Vietnamese with an array of ordnance. Nelson and Clifton proved to be excellent spirits, talking enthusiastically about the two NVA they had seen thrown from the bunker, and eager to return to the fight.

Meanwhile, on either side, Charlie and Delta companies pushed forward up parallel approaches, the former along a ridge top and the latter up a ravine. Snipers harassed Charlie company incessantly, while Delta found the ravine almost impassible and also swept by sniper fire.

Honeycutt ordered a group of engineers to cut an LZ in the jungle closer to Bravo company's now advanced position. This would greatly improve both resupply and the swift evacuation of wounded men. As the UH-1 helicopter went into a hover over the chosen site, however, the NVA opened fire with a number of machine guns. The helicopter pilot banked frantically away, causing one engineer to fall through the jungle canopy and shatter both his legs on impact.

Honeycutt ordered his forward air controller, "Dump the world on their asses. Do you hear me? Let the bastards have it." (Zaffiri, 1988, 116). In response, F105s dropped 30 500 lb bombs on the NVA positions. As the helicopter approached a second time, a RPG lashed out from the mountain slope, shattering its rotor and sending it plunging to the ground. All six engineers and four crew on board suffered severe injuries. Bravo company's men rescued them shortly before the burning helicopter exploded.

In response, the Americans unleashed the full might of their weaponry on the slopes above Bravo Company. F105s opened the proceedings with 1000 lb bombs. After this, ten howitzer batteries pounded the splintered trees and torn earth and stone with a howling fusillade of shells, marching their fire repeatedly up and down Dong Ap Bia's middle slope for half an hour. This did not conclude the fury, however. Cobra gunships arrived, fired their full complement of rockets into the mountainside, then churned the broken jungle with thousands of rounds from their miniguns. As they broke off, the F105s returned, having rearmed at their base, and slammed the same patch of terrain with more 1000 lb bombs. Only B-52s saw no use due to the nearness of American soldiers.

While engineers advanced on foot to cut an LZ in Bravo's immediate rear, the NVA halted Charlie and Delta companies well short of their jumping-off positions for the planned May 13th advance. Once again, the North Vietnamese used RPGs to good effect, firing into the treetops near Charlie company to wound 8 of its men with shrapnel and splintered wood. However, return recoilless rifle fire struck a hidden NVA ammunition cache, setting off a thunderous explosion that scattered the NVA RPG men in panic.

Confirming their elite status, the NVA did not simply remain on the defensive. That night, a raid struck Firebase Airborne, one of the five firebases established to support Operation Apache Snow with howitzers. Alpha Company of the 2/501st garrisoned this position, located on a ridge, on the fateful night of May 12-13.

A large detachment of picked sappers from the 6th NVA Regiment stealthily approached Firebase Airborne in the deep blackness of the tropical night, coming from caves located in the nearby Doi Thong hill. The most skillful of these men crawled forward and disabled the trip-flares amid the firebase's wire entanglements without setting off a single flare. Working almost silently with no tools except bamboo slivers to disable the flares, and wire cutters, the sappers cut half a dozen approaches through the wire without the American guards hearing or seeing them.

Shortly after 3:00 a.m., a sudden 82mm mortar bombardment swept the Firebase. Sappers of the K12 Sapper Battalion and supporting infantry simultaneously poured a hail of RPG rocket-propelled grenades into the perimeter, aiming accurately at many specific American defensive works. Some of the Americans jolted out of sleep only to die, while many others tumbled from their sleeping places to find a scene of confusion lit by explosions and burning wreckage. Sappers swarmed into the firebase, hurling grenades and satchel charges into the American bunkers. Any wounded man heard groaning or screaming drew several sappers, who quickly killed him with multiple shots from their AK-47s. Other sappers hosed down the American soldiers with AK-47s as they attempted to muster a defense. Flitting North Vietnamese shapes shooting rifles and throwing explosives seemed to everywhere inside the wire perimeter.

With the company commander out of action, two sergeants, Roger Barski and Kenneth Counts, finally managed to organize a defense, then a counterattack. By this time, the sappers had brought several machine guns into the firebase perimeter and set them to sweep the open ground.

Barski, Counts, and a band of men under Lieutenant Howard Pitts regained control of the firebase's northern end. Approximately 40 strong, they advanced from there, mowing down sappers by the dozen. An ad hoc unit which held a key knoll and provided illumination with mortar star-shells also contributed greatly to the successful defense, as the 101st's after-action report described: "E Company, a mortar platoon, and the 2nd and 3d Squads from the 3d Platoon, A/2-501, all which held the small knoll on the east side of the fire base, received a two prong attack from the NE and NW. The 81mm mortar platoon continued to fire illumination and HE fires throughout the conflict. [...] It was the actions of individuals of this element in braving heavy enemy fire and delivering continuous illumination and HE rounds which helped considerably to hold back the attack. Had the NVA forces gained control of this knoll and set up a base of fire into the Airborne proper, they would have been firing down the throats of the men defending the fire base." (Report, 1969).

At this point, an AC-47 Spooky gunship arrived on the scene. The ripping buzz of its miniguns echoed in the night, churning a lethal curtain of 7.62x51mm bullets through the North Vietnamese infantry attempting to move up to the sappers' aid. The sappers and infantry retreated, leaving behind 39 dead inside the perimeter and a dozen more draped grotesquely over the wire. The next day revealed numerous blood trails where the infantry dragged off their stricken comrades after the Spooky attack. The NVA inflicted remarkable damage, however, wounding 62 men – many of them badly – and killing 26 more. The Americans captured one wounded sapper alive. The after-action report went on to describe the North Vietnamese: "The attack was conceived, planned and executed in the typical, thorough fashion of a well trained sapper unit. A stealthy approach, a violent execution lasting approximately 90 minutes, and then a hasty withdrawal leaving a covering force in contact. [...] The enemy dead were well equipped with satchel charges, dressed in loin cloths or shorts, though several were completely naked. They also wore the head band to prevent sweat from getting in their eyes. They were well built, well fed husky men with fresh haircuts." (Report, 1969).

This attack naturally drew the notice of General Zais and other officers overseeing the A Shau operations. It represented yet another sign that the NVA occupied the valley in considerable numbers and showed unusual boldness in their tactics.

On Hill 937, Charlie Company of the 3/187th began their morning advance along their assigned ridge at daybreak on May 13th. Their ridge lay on the right flank of the advance, closest to the Laotian border. At first light, the men prepared their weapons and moved south, up the slopes towards the looming crown of the Crouching Beast.

For a brief interval, Charlie Company moved forward quickly and with no opposition. They covered a remarkable amount of ground, drawing parallel with Boccia's Bravo Company on the next ridge over to the east, then pulling slightly ahead. Any hopes that the bombardment had killed or driven off all the NVA soon dissipated, however, as RPGs howled in from ahead, bursting in the trees to send their lethal fountains of shrapnel earthwards. Simultaneously, NVA bunkers hidden in the ravine between the ridges along which Charlie and Bravo Companies advanced opened an enfilading fire against Charlie Company. To counter these, Honeycutt ordered Bravo Company to drop down east side of their ridge to put it between them and the bunkers, temporarily aborting their advance. An F-105 airstrike then dropped 1,000 lb bombs on the bunkers to relieve Charlie Company.

While the bombs smashed the bunkers and drove back the NVA RPG skirmishers, one fell too close to Bravo and killed a popular Swedish Minnesotan named Myles Westman. His death demoralized his comrades and sent Lieutenant Boccia into such a prolonged frenzy of anger and grief that his immediate superior, Captain Littnan, considered cashiering him on the spot. Several other men suffered wounds from their own side's bomb shrapnel.

When Boccia regained control, Bravo Company attempted to advance. Both Charlie and Bravo Companies met such stiff resistance in the following hours, however, that both stopped and eventually fell back. The North Vietnamese attacked vigorously with AK-47 fire, RPGs launched from hidden spiderholes, and grenades sent tumbling down the steep slopes to burst among the Americans.

Meanwhile, on the left flank, Delta Company struggled to the base of their jungle-choked ravine and attempted to airlift out their casualties. However, the NVA watched and, as a medevac helicopter hovered and began extracting the wounded, launched an RPG into the vulnerable craft. Shattered and burning, the helicopter fell on the men below, crushing several to death and chopping three to pieces with its rotors. The helicopter then exploded, killing several men on board.

Delta company men pulled the pilot, Lieutenant Gerald Torba, free of the wreckage, badly burned and with his left leg crushed. They would carry him with them for a time, but they eventually believed he died from his burns and placed him on a pile of dead NVA for later retrieval. Torba ultimately survived after being found alive 17 hours later by other Americans and evacuated. He lost his leg but remained in the military.

Realizing the company's vulnerability – trapped in low ground abd shocked by the crash and explosion of the helicopter in their midst – the NVA swarmed from their bunkers and spiderholes to pour down the ridges flanking Delta's ravine. Captain Luther Sanders, understanding the peril based on the greatly increased volume of enemy fire spattering down the ravine, called in an airstrike. The fighter-bombers which responded caught the NVA troops bunched in the open, and strafed them with cannon fire, strewing the ground with dead and dying Vietnamese and sending the rest fleeing back up the hill.

While all three companies attempted to push uphill, the numbers against them simply proved too great. Regardless of airstrikes and artillery, the battalion's 350 men could not overcome the fire superiority of the 1,200 or more NVA holding the high ground above them. The attack stalled bloodily again, with more men wounded.

The North Vietnamese once more showed their aggression and keen observation of the Americans' dispositions. 1st Platoon, Charlie Company began cutting an LZ on the ridge immediately behind the unit front for easier resupply and medevac. However, a platoon of NVA slipped around the flank of the leading companies and moved through the elephant grass towards the LZ site. The NVA soldiers opened fire just as an alert sentry spotted them, killing two Americans and wounding five more. 1st Platoon's commander, Lieutenant Joel Trautman, counterattacked with the support of one private, Otis Smith. Their example rallied the rest of the men and the heavy fire poured into the NVA drove them off.

By this time, Honeycutt understood clearly that he needed more men to take Hill 937. His constant, urgent demands for more troops compelled General Zais to order a second battalion, the 1/506th, known as the Currahees, to move from their current sweep near the A Sap River and support Honeycutt's 3/187th. The men moved out immediately, but a daunting cross-country trek faced them through nearly impassible terrain, and they could not hope to reach Dong Ap Bia for several days.

With more airstrikes and howitzer fire raking the mountain, the Rakkasans dug in for another night. As Honeycutt flew over the mountain in his helicopter, a North Vietnamese hailed him in English on a captured radio, referring to him by his call sign of "Blackjack" and mocking him and his men.

As first light filtered over the A Shau Valley on May 14th, "Blackjack" decided on his next moves. Aerial reconnaissance and other intelligence efforts indicated NVA reinforcements and resupply flowing in out of the North Vietnamese "safe space," Laos, just 1.2 miles distant. Hill 900, just slightly lower than Hill 937, formed a massive, jungle-covered bridge from Laos to Dong Ap Bia across which the North Vietnamese moved men and materiel almost at will. Attacking it presented just as daunting a prospect as the main hill.

Honeycutt remained keenly aware of the numerical problems and the slow progress of the reinforcing battalion towards the battle site. At the same time, he believed the NVA continued to strengthen the hill's defenses and that it would become harder, not easier, to dislodge them as time passed. He therefore resolved on a simultaneous assault by Charlie, Bravo, and Delta Companies in the hope that the NVA would prove unable to concentrate against any of the three.

A devastating, thunderous artillery barrage slammed into the Crouching Beast at dawn, preparing the way for the assault troops. Shells from the howitzers at all five firebases screamed in to blast apart tree trunks, bunkers, and NVA soldiers alike. The artillery fell silent at 6:46 precisely to make way to fighter-bomber attacks. Blasting the mountainside with both 500-pound and 1,000-pound bombs and searing it with canister after canister of napalm, the American pilots continued their runs for a whole hour. The waiting troops of the battalion saw not only trees but human figures hurled high into the air as the explosions tore through the North Vietnamese positions.

The flaming, exploding cataclysm finally ceased, and shortly before 8:00 a.m. all three companies of the assault force moved out. The troops abandoned their rucksacks and carried only water, weaponry, and ammunition for the push up the 45° slope. Almost immediately, they encountered heavy North Vietnamese fire. Soviet-made MON-100 claymore mines hanging in the trees detonated, sending lethal blasts of fragments downslope into Bravo company's leading elements and wounding several men. The MON-100, made of sheet metal, resembled a small satellite dish rather than the familiar American configuration of claymore command-detonated mine. It measured about 9.25 inches in diameter and contained 4.4 pounds of TNT.

Charlie Company enjoyed better initial success. They knocked out three bunkers on their route of march using 90mm recoilless rifles, and rapidly advanced at least 500 feet. They then started up the flank of Hill 900, with the possibility of cutting off Hill 937 from Laos tantalizingly before them. Then they encountered a second line of heavily defended bunkers.

A huge firefight erupted as Charlie Company pressed forward despite showers of grenades, blasts of AK-47 fire, and a continuous flow of RPGs. The whole slope erupted into a continuous roar of firing, and once again, the company systematically wiped out the bunkers using their recoilless rifles. They pushed past the shattered ruins, and for a brief time, the crest of Hill 900 appeared to be within their grasp.

Ultimately, the NVA managed to turn the tide with the top of Hill 90 just 120 feet distant. Treetop snipers wounded many of the advancing men, and a force of North Vietnamese counterattacked, outflanking Charlie Company and compelling them to halt lest they be overrun from the rear. Other NVA troops swarmed down from Hill 937.

Caught in a pincer maneuver by superior numbers, the Americans found themselves suddenly fighting desperately for their lives. The perilous situation for Charlie Company compelled Bravo Company to halt while Lieutenant Boccia led his platoon across the mountain face to the other company's aid. Once Boccia and his men moved clear, the other platoons advanced on an NVA bunker line. Heavy fire greeted them, which they eventually traced to numerous snipers perched in the 100-foot trees, and thus immune to the bombs and howitzer shells hitting the ground below them. The men shot the snipers out of the trees and advanced to the bunker line, finding it in ruins and the NVA defenders reduced to piles of body parts and chunks of flesh, making a body count impossible.

Delta Company also met with stiff resistance which halted them, but the NVA concentrated on Charlie Company, and in order to avoid being surrounded and wiped out, the company retreated. Honeycutt withdrew Bravo and Delta also to prevent them from being outflanked. The NVA launched a number of counterattacks against the retreating Americans, pursuing them with great vigor, and to make matters worse, two Cobra gunships attempting to support the 1/506th Currahees lost their way entirely. Wandering over the landscape, the pilots spotted Bravo Company retreating down Hill 937. Believing they were NVA moving to block 1/506th – then miles away – they hosed down their own men with minigun fire, severely wounding four. Honeycutt understandably flew into a rage, reiterating his threat to shoot down any unauthorized helicopter approaching his men. Those listening on the radio also heard him shout, "Jesus Christ! What the f*** is going on around here? This is turning into a goddamn three ring circus." (Zaffiri, 1988, 185).

Once again, the Americans carried out a skillful, well-supported assault but simply lacked the manpower to consolidate their gains. The NVA had enough men to block all three companies simultaneously and even threaten to overwhelm them. As a powerful rainstorm broke over the mountain around 5:00 p.m., the troops set up defensive positions, disgusted at having to give up their territorial gains and the overrun bunker lines.

Honeycutt, as angry as they, increased his demands for reinforcements. He received information that the 1/506th continued to approach, and that two ARVN battalions would also be added to the fight in the near future.

Turning the Tide

During the night of May 14, the NVA soldiers lit numerous cooking fires on the mountain, clearly visible from the American positions. The number of fires gave the Americans an alarming appraisal of the odds they faced, and the blazes made clear the North Vietnamese's determination to stand and fight. They cooked only every three to four days and would have simply slipped away if they did not intend to continue the struggle.

Sleeping briefly, then studying his maps, Honeycutt anticipated that the NVA would put a large number of men into the ravine between Charlie and Bravo companies, then attack both in the rear as soon as they began advancing. Recognizing the battered, exhausted state of Charlie Company, the Lieutenant Colonel withdrew them entirely from the fighting line under cover of darkness. They took up a position guarding his command post and the main forward LZ in relative safety. Alpha Company, until then serving as guards, moved up to replace them on the right.

Thinking carefully, Blackjack set up and sprang his ambush. On the morning of May 15, after the usual artillery bombardment, Alpha and Bravo companies advanced up the mountain as if for another assault. After going a short distance, however, they quietly halted and deployed facing each other, weapons pointed down into the ravine between their respective ridges.

Precisely as anticipated, large numbers of NVA soldiers in their pith helmets and light green uniforms, AK-47s at the ready, swarmed up out of the ravine on both sides. Instead of finding the Americans upslope and facing away, however, they walked into two fields of fire and came under a storm of 5.56mm and 7.62x51mm. Shocked and decimated, the NVA rushed back into the ravine for shelter, after which Honeycutt sprang the remainders of his trap. Two F-105s bombed the ravine and strafed it with 20mm cannons. Then, a rolling howitzer barrage marched up and down its length, while Alpha and Bravo companies shot any Vietnamese trying to escape the killing ground. To complete the scene, two Cobra gunships hovered slowly up the ravine, spraying every remaining sign of movement with minigun fire. The company of NVA soldiers died to a man, unable to escape the lethal low ground boxing them in.

At 1:00 p.m., Alpha and Bravo Company moved up the mountain slope to the attack. Almost immediately, they ran into heavy fire from newly dug spiderholes in fresh, unexpected positions, treetop snipers, and hastily reconstructed bunkers. The sheer numbers of NVA made it possible for them to recover quickly from each assault and prepare to meet the next in force.

Nevertheless, the Americans managed to push forward again, overrunning another bunker line, with the help of airstrikes. This continued until a Cobra gunship fired a rocket into the Bravo company command post, wounding Captain Littnan and a number of others. The NVA saw the Americans hit by their own rockets and immediately launched an aggressive attack on Bravo company. Though the attempt to envelop the company cost the NVA many lives, they forced Bravo Company to retreat.

Alpha Company's attack gained considerable ground but finally halted under fire from a sturdy bunker line. As a fierce thunderstorm descended over the scene, Alpha withdrew to their starting positions, harassed by the North Vietnamese. Bravo Company attempted another attack, but they sustained more wounded from MON-100 claymores set up to block their advance. At Honeycutt's command, both companies fell back 400 yards and established a combined defensive position together.

At this point, Honeycutt received permission to halt the attack until reinforcements arrived. During the night, an NVA sapper company attempted to repeat the success of their attack on Firebase Airborne with an assault on the Rakkasan's command post itself, but Charlie Company met them with fire from M79 grenade launchers. Shooting the grenades directly into individual sappers, the Americans caused many of them to explode blindingly as the ordnance set off the satchel charges they carried. An AC-119G gunship added to the carnage with its quadruple miniguns. In the end the decimated sappers retreated without killing or wounding a single American.

The Rakkasans enjoyed a relative respite on May 16th, remaining in their defensive positions while the 1/506th moved slowly closer. Coming from near the Laotian border, the Currahees pushed towards Hill 900 against rapidly increasing NVA resistance. The 16th witnessed them creeping closer to the battle site while airstrikes and artillery continued to rake Dong Ap Bia.

On the 17th, 1/506th moved still nearer to Hill 900, encountering stiff resistance and losing a number of wounded. Alpha Company of the 3/187th also attempted an advance after artillery and air preparation. Strong NVA counterattacks soon stopped this, and Honeycutt and Brigade headquarters agreed that on the following day, the 1/506th and 3/187th would advance simultaneously, thus hopefully reducing the pressure on both by forcing the NVA to split their available troops.

As the troops on both sides of Dong Ap Bia prepared to advance simultaneously on the morning of May 18th, prearranged airstrikes hammered the ground just ahead of them in the hopes of killing NVA there and possibly destroying their bunkers. Then, the firebases launched a barrage of CS tear gas shells intended to flush the NVA soldiers out of their spiderholes and bunker lines into the open where they made easier targets. As World War I soldiers experienced all too frequently with more lethal chemicals, gas can blow the wrong way or not reach the target, and in this case the tear gas backfired appallingly on the Americans. The artillery missed their target by a quarter-mile and managed to drop the CS gas shells directly on Alpha Company of the 3/187th. Many gas masks malfunctioned due to rain-soaked filters, causing dozens of men to begin vomiting uncontrollably. Honeycutt had requested that no CS gas be used, but 3rd Brigade had turned him down, thus creating yet another "friendly fire" incident.

Fortunately for the Americans, the following bombardment of live, high explosive shells landed accurately, shredding the ruined jungle atop Hill 937 yet again. Alpha and Delta companies moved out as soon as the shelling ceased and almost immediately ran into heavy resistance. Alpha company's officers took heavy losses and their attack fizzled out almost instantly.

Delta Company enjoyed greater success at first. Encountering a bunker line supported by trenches and carefully sited spiderholes, the men attacked vigorously using their rifles and M79 grenade launchers. A secondary explosion caused by a live grenade falling from a killed NVA soldier's hand rocked the bunker line, creating a momentary distraction for the Americans to exploit. Rushing directly up to the bunkers, the 101st men fired their M79s through the bunker firing slits point blank. Within a few furious moments, the Americans overran the bunker line and killed its defenders.

Pushing on up the slope above the bunkers, however, they encountered MON-100 Soviet claymore mines. The NVA command detonated these, wounding Captain Sanders and Lieutenant Lipscomb badly. Lieutenant Walden took over command of the whole company.

Incredibly, Delta Company pushed forward despite the claymores, machine gun fire, showers of grenades, and constant barrages of RPG rocket-propelled grenades. Coming to a particularly stubborn line of trenches, where several Americans suffered wounds and Pfc William Kirkland died, an airstrike called in by the lieutenant placed napalm directly into the trenches, roasting the NVA occupants alive.

The success of Delta Company at overrunning two bunker lines forced the NVA elsewhere on Hill 937 to fall back lest they be outflanked and surrounded. This allowed Alpha Company to advance at around noon, with the NVA pressure on their own front slackening. While this represented a success for the Americans, the Currahees of 1/506th had scarcely advanced at all, leaving the Rakkasans effectively acting on their own.

Bravo Company sent a platoon forward towards Alpha Company to bring them ammunition for their continued push towards the mountaintop. As they trekked up the slopes, however, a Cobra gunship once again sprayed them with minigun fire, killing one and wounding four more. Honeycutt, beside himself with rage at the pilot's "incompetence," roared in the radio that he wanted no more Cobras to approach the hill at all, given the sheer number of friendly fire incidents.

Delta Company's attack eventually bogged down at another bunker line. Charlie Company moved up to support, with a second platoon of the decimated, exhausted Bravo Company following them with a supply of ammunition and water. Honeycutt took to the air in a reconnaissance helicopter piloted by one "Crazy Rairdon," flying dangerously low through a hail of machine gun fire to observe the situation. Observing from his helicopter, Honeycutt called in airstrikes and artillery bombardment on the bunkers and trenches he could see. When these arrived, he provided data allowing the distant artillery crews to adjust their aim precisely onto their targets.

At this point, Charlie Company, bringing up ammunition and water for the front line, came under fire from an adjacent ridgeline. The 1/506th claimed to be on this ridge, but when Honeycutt and Rairdon flew low over it, they saw the pith helmets of NVA soldiers below them. AK-47 fire riddled the skin of their helicopter but struck nothing essential. Clearly, the 1/506th had not advanced to where the plan called for it to be, supporting the flank of the Rakkasans.

As the helicopter swooped away from the NVA-infested ridge, Honeycutt ordered the 1/506th to pop smoke to mark their position. The smoke revealed them a quarter-mile away, far too distant to provide any help to the assault companies with the dense, North Vietnamese held jungle terrain in between. Nevertheless, when Honeycutt radioed Captain Harkins, now commanding a mix of Delta and Charlie Company platoons on the upper flanks of the mountain, the captain thought he could reach the crest unsupported. Thus, Honeycutt landed at the command post LZ and started the climb up the mountain with a few of his staff, intending to take part in the final assault. He bore a Colt CAR-15, a short-barreled M16 variant. Along the way, he and his five-man party stumbled on a group of NVA closing in on the LZ Bravo company had established to medevac the wounded. A short, vicious firefight at point blank range ensued, during which Honeycutt personally killed three NVA and one of his officers killed four more. The North Vietnamese faded back into the jungle and Honeycutt radioed a warning to the LZ.

Before the final assault on the hilltop began, a tremendous thunderstorm downpour swept onto the mountain. With the jungle stripped and shattered by days of ceaseless bombardment, the red earth turned into deep, sucking mud in a few moments, up to three feet deep in places. Advance became an impossibility as the rain continued and lightning lashed the crown of Dong Ap Bia, filling the air with slamming discharges of thunder.

With the attack broken off by the weather, Honeycutt ordered a retreat at 2:32 p.m. Charlie and Delta companies fell back while Alpha Company provided covering fire and then retreated in turn. Around half the men now had suffered wounds, and nearly all officers wounded or killed.

When the storm ceased, the 1/506th resumed their advance. With triple-canopy jungle still in place at their location, the ground did not turn to muck and the men moved forward rapidly until they encountered a bunker line. This briefly halted Alpha Company until Lieutenant Robert Schmitz outflanked the bunkers with his platoon. Though Schmitz took a serious pelting of shrapnel from an RPG round which necessitated his evacuation, the platoon swiftly cleared 10 bunkers and a large number of spiderholes and trenches. Alpha and Bravo companies managed to push almost to the crest of Hill 900 before digging in for the night under sniper fire from the NVA.

In the meantime, at the headquarters of General Abrams, General Zais received approval to continue the attack. He also met Secretary of State William Pierce Rogers, then visiting Vietnam. To Zais' astonishment, Rogers knew nothing of the American political policy of keeping Laos and Cambodia off-limits to American action. Rogers vowed strenuously to do something about the situation, and nothing ever came of his promises.

Rogers

The evening's politicking did not end there. A second battalion of the 506th Airborne Infantry Regiment, the 2/506th, made its way as rapidly as possible across the A Shau Valley to relieve the exhausted, damaged 3/187th. Lieutenant Colonel Gene Sherron of the 2/506th arrived at the LZ by helicopter to confer with Honeycutt. Shortly thereafter, General Zais also arrived.

Zais planned originally to withdraw the 3/187th entirely, including Honeycutt, to remove them from the ongoing struggle for Hill 937. He did this not as a punishment for failure but to provide them a respite. However, Honeycutt expressed outrage at being removed from the hill precisely at the moment it seemed certain to fall. Accordingly, Zais agreed to helicopter in Alpha Company of the 2/506th under Captain William "Bill" Womble instead, placing the company under Honeycutt's direct command.

With preparations for the final assault underway, the Americans spent May 19th readying their multiple battalion attack on Hill 937. Airstrikes slammed the hill again and again, aiming at the bunkers and other defenses along the planned approach routes. Meanwhile, a fleet of helicopters brought a full battalion of South Vietnamese – the 2/3 ARVN – to Firebase Currahee. From there, they moved into an attack position southeast of the Crouching Beast, reaching their jumping-off point with no difficulty. The 2/501st ferried in to a new LZ northeast of the hill and also assumed a posture of readiness.

While these fresh troops arrived, 1/506th started their advance up Hill 900 at 10:00 a.m. on the morning of May 19th. During the next three hours, they systematically outflanked and destroyed several large clusters of bunkers, killing the NVA inside, and took the hilltop, at a cost of 19 wounded. A command bunker atop Hill 900 also fell into American hands, along with many documents.

With Hill 900 taken by 1:00 p.m., elements of the 1/506th pushed forward towards Hill 937. 2nd Platoon, Charlie Company under Lieutenant Timothy LeClair moved across a small stream towards a narrow ridge rising towards Hill 937 and came under heavy fire from multiple bunkers. LeClair, a hectoring, seemingly gung-ho type, panicked completely after ordering his men forward and cowered in a shell hole for a time. After several minutes, however, he changed to a mood of reckless courage, leaping to his feet and charging forward, only to be shot dead by an NVA soldier.

The other platoons moved up to support 2nd Platoon. While the firefight continued, Pfc. Paul Skaggs rose to his feet and moved forward. The only firearm Skaggs carried consisted of a 1911 .45 caliber pistol, but he had also hung a large satchel stuffed to the brim with grenades around his neck. Sauntering to the first bunker, he threw a handful of grenades in, then, after they exploded, leaped inside and shot the NVA sprawled on the floor with his 1911. He repeated this again and again until he wiped out the four main bunkers and the advance resumed.

With the bunkers now cleared, 1/506th moved forward and assumed their assault positions. Each company and platoon set up its defensive perimeter for the night and waited for the four-pronged assault planned for the morrow. Atop Hill 937, the Pride of Ho Chi Minh also awaited the following day with iron resolve. Using a captured American radio, a North Vietnamese hailed Honeycutt personally, "When you come up the mountain in the morning, Blackjack, we will be waiting for you. All of your men are going to die. Can you hear me, Blackjack? All will die!" (Zaffiri, 1988, 273).

Aggressive to the last, the NVA launched several small preemptive attacks on the Americans in the pre-dawn darkness. A squad of NVA soldiers bombarded Honeycutt's command post with RPGs at 5:30 a.m., then escaped. A North Vietnamese soldier approached Alpha Company, 1/506th, pretending that he wished to surrender. Once within 30 feet of the Americans, he detonated a claymore mine in his backpack, blowing himself to a mist of shredded flesh and wounding four American soldiers badly. Other units suffered grenade attacks or sniper fire.

Airstrikes delivered bombs and napalm to the top of Hill 937, followed by a steady, rapid howitzer bombardment, for a total of 3.5 hours as daylight arrived on May 20th. At 10:00 a.m., the Americans and ARVN began a simultaneous advanced up Hill 937 from all directions. The wreckage of the jungle above them still burned from the airstrikes and artillery preparation, trailing black smoke into the morning sky.

As the men climbed the scarred, muddy, blackened slopes, dead silence met them. Honeycutt personally piloted the reconnaissance helicopter, accompanied by a major, watching his men's advance from a low hover.

The troops converging up the mountainsides from all points of the compass found a bunker line ringing the hilltop. It proved to be deserted. Destroying the bunkers, they moved on to a second line. At this point, the air suddenly filled with blasts of rifle, machine-gun, and RPG fire as the surviving NVA, lurking silently until then in slit trenches, struck.

With just 75 yards to go to the hilltop, Honeycutt urged his men on vigorously. A series of large, A-frame bunkers, too tough to be knocked out even by the heavy strikes on the hill, opened fire until destroyed with 90mm recoilless rifle fire. As Sp.4 Edward Merjil destroyed two bunkers by firing his M79 grenade launcher directly through their firing slit, the men of 2nd Platoon, Charlie Company, 3/187th became the first Americans to reach the summit of Hill 937.

As more of Charlie Company reached the hilltop and began reducing bunkers, killing the occupants of 10 bunkers in 15 minutes, the North Vietnamese finally began to disintegrate. Larger and larger groups began to flee down the west side of Hill 937, through the saddle between Hill 917 and Hill 900, towards the safety of Laos. Even still, most of them retained enough discipline to carry their weapons with them.

Bravo Company moved to block the fleeing soldiers, and 81mm mortars pounded those caught between the hill and the blocking force. Arthur Wiknik described the scene: "Thirty paralyzing minutes passed as I watched the assault continue. The GIs made tremendous progress, killing the enemy in their bunkers where many had chosen to stay and die. Scores of other NVA ran off the western slope toward the Laotian border, a mile away. The fleeing enemy could easily be seen from the air where our helicopters directed a wall of artillery, mortars, airstrikes, and automatic weapons fire on top of them." (Wiknik, 2009, 47).

One group of NVA, with notable courage and professionalism, concentrated against Bravo company's blocking line and blew a hole through it with RPGs. Once through the line, they turned in both directions and attacked the blocking troops from the rear, attempting to open the gap wider to allow more of their comrades to escape. The Americans beat them off, however, killing 20-25 of them at the loss of 5 wounded.

Not all of the NVA chose to flee. In some areas, entire platoons of NVA soldiers left their bunkers, spiderholes, and trenches and charged the Americans head-on. These silent, eerie Vietnamese equivalents of Japanese banzai charges added an additional toll of wounded Americans and dead NVA to the already corpse-choked hilltop and slopes. Scores of NVA charged Bravo Company, 1/506th, as they moved up the slopes to finish clearing their sector. The Americans set up two M60 machine guns and mowed each group down, yet more kept coming until dead and dying men carpeted the ground in front of the twin automatic weapons.

One of the last actions of the Battle of Hamburger Hill came when the Americans killed eight NVA who had chained themselves upright to trees, with slogans such as "Defeat the Americans, here we make a stand!" pinned to their shirts. The battle sputtered to a halt as the final defenders died and those able and willing to escape in the direction of Laos slipped past the Americans and made their getaway.

The Americans paid with 70 dead for the hill, along with 372 wounded, though final figures vary. The claimed body count of NVA stood somewhere between 633 and 699. However, more may have died, since the Americans found many trenches filled with a jumble of severed arms, legs, heads, torsos, entrails, and chunks of flesh after a week of ferocious bombardment, making a precise count extremely difficult. The entire mountaintop proved to be a honeycomb of tunnels, connecting underground bunkers, storage rooms, command centers, armories, and even a large hospital.

The 3/187th, which bore the brunt of the fighting throughout, helicoptered out on the following day, May 21st. All of the survivors received several weeks of rest and relaxation at Eagle Beach, a converted pumping station. MACV rotated Honeycutt and all other surviving ranking officers out of command within a month, in accordance with their peculiar Vietnam War custom of completely rotating combat commanders every six months.

The Americans built a road up to the summit of the mountain and placed a number of tanks and APCs there, anticipating an NVA counterattack. As fate would have it, that attack did not come until after MACV rotated General Zais out and replaced him with General John Wright. Wright, unfamiliar with the situation, withdrew all troops from Dong Ap Bia by June 5th, igniting another political firestorm of controversy.

With NVA soldiers reoccupying the Crouching Beast shortly afterward, Wright launched Operation Montgomery Rendezvous in the A Shau region starting on June 8th and continuing through August 15th in an effort to protect Hue. In a series of sweeps, the Americans killed 393 NVA soldiers at a cost of 87 casualties. He planned to garrison a powerful base camp in the A Shau to deny it to the North Vietnamese, but President Nixon's drawdown of forces made this impossible, leaving the jungle-clad valley permanently in the possession of the soldiers of Ho Chi Minh.

The Legacy of Hamburger Hill

Hamburger Hill is almost unique among the individual battles of the Vietnam War for the persistent, long-term controversy and negativity surrounding it. A storm of media recriminations began long before the encounter developed far enough to pass judgment, and the dispute spread to the halls of Congress and the Senate. It entered the annals of history through numerous media reports and eventually popular culture via a feature film starring Anthony Barile and Don Cheadle.

The press stridently condemned the action as pointless butchery and all American military commanders as arrogant, incompetent buffoons without exception. Senator Edward Kennedy said in the Senate, "I feel it is both senseless and irresponsible to continue to send our young men to their deaths to capture hills and positions that have no relation to ending this conflict. […] The assault on 'Hamburger Hill' is only symptomatic of a mentality and a policy that requires immediate attention. American boys are too valuable to be sacrificed for a false sense of military pride."

While some veterans agreed, others disagreed with the Senator's speech vigorously. Captain Charles Littnan of Bravo Company, who led the men at the forefront of some of the worst fighting and therefore personally experienced the direct results of Honeycutt's and Zais' command decisions, later remarked in an interview, "After his statement in the Senate, Kennedy went to the top of my all-time shit list. What he said about Zais was really despicable." (Zaffiri, 1988, 311).

What can be said with certainty about the battle, at least from a tactical perspective, is both sides fought the encounter with great bravery. Some young draftees and a few older veterans succumbed to panic on the American side, but most of the American soldiers fought doggedly, and some with cool professionalism and heroic resolve. For their part, the NVA showed great valor, sometimes to a suicidal degree, matching some banzai charge actions of the Imperial Japanese in World War II.

The Americans also applied tactics in a professional manner throughout. While some myths about the battle portray Lieutenant Colonel Honeycutt as throwing his troops forward recklessly without support, he actually made maximum use of support by Cobra gunships, F105 airstrikes, AC-47 "Spooky" gunships, and the howitzer batteries of five separate firebases throughout the engagement. For their part, the NVA's tactics remained aggressive and professional throughout. Their RPG users, in particular, made excellent use of the terrain by firing their rockets into the branches to produce a lethal downward shower of shrapnel and shattered, razor-sharp wood fragments. Though limited by a relative lack of heavy weapons, they made full use of surprise, interlocking fields of fire, well laid out defensive positions, snipers, and more.

From the American perspective, the bloody, inconclusive fighting of the first days of the battle resulted neither from a lack of professionalism nor of tactical failures on the part of Honeycutt. The 101st Airborne soldiers used their weapons to the maximum possible advantage. Honeycutt's methods remained correct and he utilized the full weight of supporting firepower repeatedly to support the troops under his command. That a bloody stalemate resulted was simply because of insufficient soldiers on the American side. The NVA 29th Regiment severely outnumbered the battalion initially at Honeycutt's disposal. In effect, four companies could not achieve the objective, whereas four battalions could and did in the course of little more than a day.

Even with colossal firepower in support and skilled use of the troops available, one battalion of the 101st could not defeat the NVA while attacking uphill, heavily outnumbered and facing long-prepared defensive positions being fanatically defended. That they nevertheless inflicted tremendous casualties on the North Vietnamese clearly emerges from the speed with which the larger number of troops in the last stage of the battle systematically overran the NVA positions despite continued resistance.

While many of the soldiers complained about Honeycutt at the time, most recognized later, free of the heat of the action, that his leadership won the battle. Lieutenant Frank Boccia, whose own hot-tempered personality clashed frequently with that of Honeycutt, had little personal liking for his commanding officer. Nevertheless, long after leaving the service, he called the Lieutenant Colonel "a helluva a fighting soldier" and elaborated on his grudging respect for Honeycutt: "I wasn't paid to love or even like him. [...] No one else, no other officer I have known, could have gained victory at Dong Ap Bia. The battalion was, for the most part, blessed with excellent junior officers, captains and lieutenants, and we did our jobs well, but we would not—could not—have achieved what we did without his leadership and his fierce, unyielding will to defeat the enemy. [...] a truer measure of how he is viewed is that in 2012 the Hamburger Hill Chapter of the Rakkasans voted to change our name to the Weldon F Honeycutt/Hamburger Hill Chapter." (Boccia, 2013, 4).

Honeycutt could not refuse the order to attack and requested reinforcements urgently throughout the action, though his ground troops had no way to know this at the time. This then raises the question of whether General Melvin Zais mishandled the battle at the operational level by not greatly reinforcing the 3/187th quickly. After a day or two, it must have been obvious that the Rakkasans faced a numerous, well-entrenched, zealously resolute enemy. Their heavy losses despite massive support indicated one thing clearly: they lacked the numbers to take Hill 937. Once reinforcements arrived, the NVA succumbed almost immediately.

In the final analysis, responsibility for the Hamburger Hill situation lay with restraints imposed on American forces from above, but given their palpable ignorance of tactics, strategy, weaponry, and military history, none of them likely ever realized this, however. Clear arguments can be made that the Americans should not have intervened in what amounted to a Vietnamese civil war at all, but once the government did, it refused to take the fight to North Vietnamese territory with the full power of the American military. General William Westmoreland provided a clear perspective on Hamburger Hill's tactics compared to the Vietnam strategy overall when he stated, "Honeycutt's tactics at Hamburger Hill were aggressive, a feature of American tactics throughout the war. Aggressive tactics may produce sharp initial casualties, but they save lives in the long run, for in a protracted battle, as in a protracted war, casualties inevitably accumulate. Allowed to drag on, the Vietnam War as a whole illustrates this point." (Westmoreland, 1976, 152).

Had the military been given more leeway to pursue victory through an offensive strategy, actions like Hamburger Hill would have been unnecessary. Bombing the North vigorously would have quickly eroded the nation's ability to fight, and allowing American forces to enter Cambodia and Laos to smash the NVA there and cut off their lines of reinforcement and supplies would have swiftly eliminated the constant risk of a large-scale invasion of South Vietnam from the west.

With Laos as an arbitrarily assigned "safety zone" for the North Vietnamese, however, the only way to deal with NVA aggression lay in meeting them on ground of their choosing. With a Laotian operational area, even had the NVA 29th Regiment occupied Hill 937, the Americans could have readily surrounded it, cutting it off from the strong reinforcements flowing in from Laos nightly. From there, the Americans could have avoided a direct assault on the hill, simply hammering the NVA with bombardment until their destruction. Since the hill lay only 1.2 miles from the Laotian border, however, the Americans had no choice but to assault the hill or risk the NVA 29th Regiment escaping or attacking Hue, as described by Captain Gerald Hawkins of Alpha Company, 3/187th: "If we had it to do over again, we would likely do the same thing. We were there to fight soldiers. We [...] decided that it was better to fight them where they were than to allow them to get down to a populated area like Hue. There was a tremendous effort on the part of Honeycutt and everyone else to use Tac Air and indirect fire. To a lot of people the big thing was the fact that we didn't use B-52s. But to do so, we would have had to pull back, and they would have gotten away." (Zaffiri, 1988, 305-306).

Perhaps Honeycutt bears some blame, if blame is to be leveled, for attacking aggressively before his reinforcements arrived, but the longer he delayed, the more time the 29th Regiment had to reinforce, resupply, and dig in. Perhaps Zais shoulders some culpability for not reinforcing Honeycutt faster, but he in turn faced limited information and the difficulties of moving men rapidly in the appalling terrain and weather of the A Shau Valley.

The Vietnam War, of course, would continue to drag on for many more years to come, consuming both lives and livelihoods on all sides. Hubert Humphrey, Johnson's Vice President and the establishment candidate, would go on to lose the tightly contested 1968 election to Richard M. Nixon. Nixon, convinced that further casualties on the scale of Tet would sink his administration as surely as they had sunk Johnson's, adopted a policy of "Vietnamization," gradually withdrawing American combat troops and replacing them with resources and training to enhance the size and effectiveness of South Vietnam's military. In the short term, this policy was reasonably successful; even as American troop numbers in Vietnam declined, the SVA (with large-scale American air support) managed to turn back a North Vietnamese offensive in 1972, and in 1973, the conclusion of the Paris Peace Accords produced a case-fire between North and South, setting the stage for the final withdrawal of all American forces in South Vietnam.

In the longer term, however, as both Nixon and Henry Kissinger well understood, the peace deal simply created a "decent interval" between American withdrawal and communist victory. In

April 1975, a final NVA offensive captured Saigon, and the Vietnam War was finally over.

Online Resources

Other books about Vietnam by Charles River Editors

Other books about Hamburger Hill on Amazon

Bibliography

Boccia, Frank. *The Crouching Beast.* Jefferson, 2013.

Boian, Major Kelly. *Major General Melvin Zais and Hamburger Hill.* Washington, 2012.

Kennedy, Edward M. "Hamburger Hill Speech." *Senator Kennedy Speeches.* Edward M. Kennedy Institute. Online. May 20, 1969. https://www.emkinstitute.org/resources/hamburger-hill-speech

Report, After Action. "SAPPER Attack On Fsb Airborne – 13 May 1969." 2nd Brigade, 101st Airborne Division. July 29th, 1969. Web.

https://alphaavengers.com/firebase-airborne.htm

Westmoreland, William. *A Soldier Reports.* New York, 1976.

Wiknik, Arthur. *Nam Sense: Surviving Vietnam with the 101st Airborne Division.* Philadelphia, 2009.

Woodruff, Mark. *Unheralded Victory: The Defeat of the Viet Cong and the North Vietnamese Army, 1961-1973.* New York, 2005.

Yarborough, Thomas. *A Shau Valor: American Combat Operations in the Valley of Death, 1963-1971.*

Zaffiri, Samuel. *Hamburger Hill: The Brutal Battle for Dong Ap Bia, May 11-20, 1969.* New York, 1988.

Free Books by Charles River Editors

We have brand new titles available for free most days of the week. To see which of our titles are currently free, click on this link.

Discounted Books by Charles River Editors

We have titles at a discount price of just 99 cents everyday. To see which of our titles are currently 99 cents, click on this link.

Printed in Great Britain
by Amazon